Fun Is Contagious

by Charles R. Swindoll

ZondervanPublishingHouse
Grand Rapids, Michigan

A Division of HarperCollins*Publishers*

Fun Is Contagious: How to Help Your Family Lighten Up
Copyright © 1990, 1995 by Charles R. Swindoll, Inc.

Requests for information should be addressed to:
    Zondervan Publishing House
    Grand Rapids, Michigan 49530

ISBN 0-310-20078-4

Fun Is Contagious is an excerpt from chapter 9 of *Growing Wise in Family Life* by Charles R. Swindoll (Portland, Ore.: Multnomah Press, 1988).

Cover design by DesignTeam, Brian L. Fowler

Printed in the United States of America
95 96 97 98 99 00 / ❖ DP / 10 9 8 7 6 5 4 3 2 1

Fun Is
Contagious

A hurry-up lifestyle results in a throw-away culture. Things that should be lasting and meaningful are sacrificed on the altar of the temporary and superficial.

The major fallout in such a setting is the habit of viewing relationships casually. This cavalier attitude cripples society in various ways:

- Friends walk away instead of work through.
- Partnerships dissolve rather than solve.
- Neighbors no longer visit and relax together. They erect stone walls and exist on isolated islands.
- The aged are resented, not honored.
- Husbands and wives divorce rather than persevere.

- Children are brushed aside rather than nourished; used and abused rather than cherished and cultivated.

Caught in the vortex of all this, the most common response is to become negative and pessimistic. Everything begins to look dark. We start anticipating failure, impossibilities, and inevitable doom. We become rigid, much too serious. We start focusing on what *isn't* going well, and our whole frame of reference, to use Bunyan's vivid analogy, takes on the likeness of the "Slough of Despond." Indifference pokes a slow leak in our boat as Intensity and Anxiety climb aboard. How difficult it is to remain positive and encouraged in such a dismal context . . . yet how essential!

I heard recently about a man who was driving through North Carolina. As he approached one of the little towns nestled in the mountains, he noticed a large sign near the city limits marker. It read:

> WE UNDERSTAND THAT A SERIOUS RECESSION IS SUPPOSED TO HAPPEN THIS YEAR, BUT WE'VE DECIDED NOT TO PARTICIPATE.

I love it! With an attitude like that, the place becomes an oasis of hope and joy in a desert of depression.

Let me encourage you to adopt a similar mindset in your family. Let's stop taking our cues from the morning paper and the evening news. Let's decide not to be influenced by those grim statistics! I'm tired of the pessimism that dominates even the weather report. How about a switch? Instead of remembering that tomorrow will have a 20 percent chance of rain, what's wrong with thinking about the 80 percent chance of sunshine?

Call me crazy if you like (you won't be the first), but I am more convinced than ever that attitudes shape just about everything we do. Not facts, not a group of so-called authorities. Not some big, thick book spelling the demise of civilization ... but *attitudes*. When those attitudes get refocused on God's power and His incredible purposes for living, hang on to your socks! Instead of running from each other in our relationships, we would be running toward one another. Before we realized it, people would become more important to us than status, fame, or fortune.

I believe it was writer Christopher Morely who said that if everybody had only five minutes to live, every phone booth in the world would be occupied by someone. Each would be sending out final words of affection and affirmation.

I may have questioned that before I endured an earthquake. Living here in southern California, you never know when "the big one" will hit. Little tremors and rock 'n' rollers keep us wondering. On October 1, 1987, I was in my study early in the morning. Suddenly, the movement of the floor gave me this strange sensation. Doors started to bump and windows rattled as an awful lot of shaking was going on. Within seconds, I was partially covered with books from the shelves above my head. My desk lamp rocked back and forth. I stumbled across the room to stand in a doorway as the thought flashed through my mind, *If this isn't "The Big One," I can't imagine what IT will be like!* As you know, it wasn't. We still have it to look forward to. It's supposed to happen each year, but I've decided not to participate!

Guess the very first thing I did when the shaking calmed down. Like E.T., I picked up the phone and called home. First, I checked to see if Cynthia, Cols, and Chuck were okay. I then made two more calls ... one to our son and his wife, Curt and Deb, and the other to our daughter and her husband, Charissa and Byron (mainly to check on the grandkids).

Relationships! When the quake hit, I never once thought, *I wonder who the church will get as my replacement.* Or, *Did we pick up the dry cleaning yesterday?* Or, *We probably ought to cancel our subscription to* Newsweek. Or, *Shoot! I forgot to get the car washed.* No way! My entire focus was on those people who bear my name, who complete the loop in my family circle.

Relationships! Never sell them short. If we'll slow down the hurry-up lifestyle for a moment and pause to catch our breath, we'll realize the need to call a halt to our throwaway culture.

FLEXIBILITY: IT IS ESSENTIAL

Uptight families cease to function properly. When Dad is tense and Mom is irritable, the kids have no trouble deciphering the message: Shut up and don't mess around. What happens down deep inside is tragic. Relationships break down. Feelings start getting internalized and confused. Negotiations are strained. Fear builds up as tension mounts. Communication is finally reduced to looks, frowns, shrugs, sarcastic jabs, and put-downs. Cooperation and teamwork fall by the wayside. Extremes emerge—long periods of silence periodically interrupted by shouting matches. Far from a haven of rest, such a home becomes a hell on earth.

FLEXIBILITY IN THE FAMILY SCENE

I offer no "series of steps" that will ultimately lead to a flexible family. I'm not writing of some sterile, theoretical technique but rather of a relational attitude. Wisdom, remember, must be given room to flow. It cannot be reduced to analytical formulas or computer programs. Growing wise in family life is a daily process, a trial-and-error, learn-as-you-go series of discoveries that has little to do with rigid rules and regulations ... and everything to do with attitudes and actions.

My message is this: In order to grow, mature, and flourish, everyone needs room; let's provide plenty of it.

Watching other families over the years has confirmed what I've discovered in my own: The two entrenched enemies of flexibility are Hurry and Rigidity. Each results in family tension. Each, therefore, must be exposed.

WHAT'S THE HURRY?

The older I get, the more I appreciate the benefits of taking time. Woodwork done slowly and meticulously by a craftsman is beautiful and able to endure the test of the elements. Art—whether musical compositions, needlework, sculpture, or painting—requires time and attention to detail. Even the cultivation of our walk with God or some ministry skill requires a great deal of time to develop.

The psalmist realized this when he wrote, "Be still, and know that I am God" (Psalm 46:10, NKJV). The Hebrew does not suggest standing around and letting your mind wander—not that kind of being still. Rather, it means "Let go; relax." The New American Standard renders this, "Cease striving." What a timely admonition!

If all this is true of other realms and responsibilities, it is certainly applicable to the home and family. Children were not created to be "jerked up" (as my mother used to put it), but to be cared for with gentleness and attention to detail. They require time ... lots of it. Not all of it needs to be supervised, however.

Perhaps the best way to describe my early childhood world of play is with the word *relaxed*. Lots of friends in the neighborhood. Sandlot football down at the end of Quince Street in East Houston on an open field adjacent to St. Andrew's Methodist Church. Endless and exhausting hours of one-on-one or "horse" over at Eugene's house—with Freddie and Bruce—as the four of us shot hoops against the garage backboard. Then there was always "Hide 'n' Seek" and "Kick the Can"—until suppertime. Weekends found me playing Cowboys and Indians, making scooters out of beat-up roller skates, running races and relays down the street, shooting my BB gun in the woods down by the creek, and messing around with crawdads after a rain.

Plenty of time to grow up ... easygoing, relaxing hours.

In the summer, there were family reunions down below Palacios at my granddaddy's little bay cabin, plus fishing, floundering, crabbing, swimming, driving the tractor, making rafts out of toesacks and old inner tubes, seining for bait, and eating. My—*did we eat*! Fresh shrimp, crab gumbo, fried gulf trout, barbecued beef cooked on chicken wire stretched over an open pit of hickory coals, freshly plucked watermelon, big brown eggs (laid that very morning), thick slab bacon, homemade biscuits, gravy, hand-cranked ice cream . . . *I gotta stop!*

Best of all, my brother, sister, and I were given room to be kids. Just kids. I went to school barefoot until the fourth grade (when Wanda Ragland and I fell madly in love), and I was still playing cops and robbers in junior high. Nobody hurried me to grow up. I suppose everybody figured it would just happen. I can still remember one hot summer afternoon sitting on the curb in torn blue jeans, licking a Popsicle, and thinking, *This is the life!* I had finished mowing the grass, putting out the trash, mopping the bathroom floor, and throwing my paper route (my major chores), and was about to head down to the church with my well-worn football to play until my daddy whistled, signaling supper.

I was just a kid. No big expectations drove me to excel or achieve. Life was allowed to run its own course back then, like a lazy river working its way down from the slopes to the sea. No big deal, no adult pressure to perform, just down-home, easy livin', fun, growin'-up stuff. And plenty of time. A lingering, relaxed childhood was mine to enjoy.

No longer, it seems. Forty years removed from my laid-back lifestyle, there is a new youngster in our city streets. Have you noticed? Perhaps I'm overly sensitive because I've read David Elkind's splendid book *The Hurried Child*, with the provocative subtitle, *Growing Up Too Fast Too Soon*.[1] On the cover is a little girl, not more than eleven or twelve ... with earrings (pierced ears, of course), plucked eyebrows, carefully applied cosmetics, teased and feathered hair, and exquisite jewelry. I've looked at that picture dozens of times, and on each occasion I see more. She bears the look of bewildered inno-cence—almost like a helpless calf being pushed to slaughter. She's afraid, but can't say so; it wouldn't be chic. She's into a role that deprives her the freedom to be simply a child. The problem? She is being hurried... like so many children and adolescents today. The luxury of childhood is no longer an option.

She reminds me of the seven-year-old whom Susan Ferraro mentioned in an article titled "Hotsy Totsy." It was the little girl's birthday party: ice cream and cake, a donkey poster with twelve tails waiting to be pinned, a door prize, the works:

> Ooh, sighed seven-year-old Melissa as she opened her first present. It was

Calvin Klein jeans. "Aah," she gasped as the second box revealed a bright new top from Gloria Vanderbilt. There were Christian Dior undies from grandma—a satiny little chemise and matching bloomer bottoms—and mother herself had fallen for a marvelous party outfit from Yves St. Laurent. Melissa's best friend gave her an Izod sports shirt, complete with alligator emblem...[2]

It's not the clothes. It's not those silly brand names that bug me. It's the message they announce. It's the subtle hurry-up woven through those threads and styles. It's the subliminal strokes and sensations a child in the second grade can wear but isn't equipped to handle.

The media isn't going to be outdone, either. Music, books, films, and of course, television increasingly portray the young as precocious and seductive. Kids are given scripts and scenes that present them in more or less explicit sexual and manipulative situations. "Such portrayals," writes Elkind, "force children to think they should act grown up before they are ready." This is certainly true in movies like *Little Darlings* where the two principals—teenaged girls— are in competition as to who will lose her virginity first. And I think I'll gag if I hear again "Take Your Time (Do It Right)" or "Do That to Me One More Time."

I'm no expert, understand, just a father

and a concerned observer. From what I've read and heard on the subject, I understand that emotions and feelings are the most complex and intricate part of development. They have their own timing and rhythm and cannot be hurried. Children can grow up fast in some ways, but not in others. It is tough enough with nobody pushing, but I'm convinced it's bewildering, even confusing, when children's behavior and appearance are hurried to speak "adult" while their insides cry "child." It simply isn't fair!

One of America's most outstanding high school quarterbacks was written up in *Sports Illustrated* a while ago. His name is Todd Marinovich. His record of passing yardage (9,914) is all-time tops. His senior year, he threw for more yards than Jim Kelley or Dan Marino or John Elway did in theirs. Of 104 Division 1-A colleges and universities, no less than 100 of them were jumping through the hoop to have this young phenom. USC eventually snagged him as their number one quarterback. The pros must already be salivating. We're talking *franchise*.

But before we get too impressed, let's back away a few feet, step into the time tunnel, and relive how this young fella, not yet twenty years old, arrived at this so-called enviable moment. It is a mouth-opening, mind-boggling account of parental fanaticism. Todd's dad, Marv, has been the primary force behind the boy's life. Trudi, his mother, has also cooperated. The article from which I quote has a telling title, "Bred to Be a Superstar."

> What's fascinating about Marinovich, a 6'4½", 212-pound lefthanded redhead, is that he is, in a real sense, America's first test-tube athlete. He has never eaten a Big Mac or an Oreo or a Ding Dong. When he went to birthday parties as a kid, he would take his own cake and ice cream to avoid sugar and refined white flour. He would eat homemade catsup, prepared with honey. He did consume beef but not the kind injected with hormones. He ate only unprocessed dairy products. he teethed on frozen kidney. When Todd was one month old, Marv was already working on his son's physical conditioning. He stretched his hamstrings. Pushups were next. Marv invented a game in which Todd would try to lift a medicine ball onto a kitchen counter. Marv also put him on a balance beam. Both activities grew easier when Todd learned to walk. There was a football in Todd's crib from day one . . .
>
> Eventually Marv started gathering experts to work on every aspect of Todd's physical condition—speed, agility, strength, flexibility, quickness, body control, endurance, nutrition. He found one to improve Todd's peripheral vision. He enlisted a throwing coach and a motion coach and a psychologist. These

days 13 different experts are donating their time in the name of science.

Tom House, the pitching coach for the Texas Rangers and a computer whiz, has analyzed Todd's form and found that while his balance is perfect, his arm is 4.53 inches too low throughout his delivery. Todd, who listens to everyone, is working on it. This Team Marinovich is the creation of Marv, who was a two-way lineman and a captain at USC in 1962, a marginal pro in the AFL with the Raiders and a sometime assistant coach for the Raiders, the Rams, the Cardinals and the Hawaiians of the defunct WFL.

Though Marv owns an athletic research center—a sort of high-tech gym—his true occupation has been the development of his son, an enterprise that has yet to produce a monetary dividend. And the Marinovich marriage ended last year after 24 years. "All Marv has done," says a friend, "is give up his entire life for Todd."

Which is fine with Marv. Father and son now live in a one-bedroom apartment. Todd has the bedroom, and Marv sleeps on the sofa in the living room. On weekends Todd visits Trudi, who has moved back in with her parents in Newport Beach.

"I think I'm a tyrant," says Marv. "But I think you have to be to succeed. The best thing about it is my relationship with my son. We wanted to have the healthiest possible mom and the healthiest possible child. It's fanatical, but I don't know if you can be a great success without being a fanatic." He pauses and then continues, "I suppose it was a little overdone."[3]

That, ladies and gents, is the understatement of the year! I cannot help but wonder if Todd will someday miss having been a child.

Scripture clearly states, "There is an appointed time for everything" (Ecclesiastes 3:1, NASB). *How about time to be a child?* How about time to grow up slowly, carefully, yes, even protected, and dare I add, a little naive? How about time to "speak as a child, think as a child, reason as a child" (1 Corinthians 13:11, NASB)? It will take a lot of effort to make that happen. For a few, it is worth it to go against the trend and allow your children the joy of childhood—encouraging them simply to be what they are. But for most, it is too big a hassle. Maybe it's because we're too busy being what we're not and pushing our kids to do the same. Let's back off and start having fun again! Let's return to the psalmist's counsel to relax . . . to cease struggling.

Flexibility, folks, doesn't come easy! You and I are surrounded by peers who tend to pressure us by making what I call hurry-up comments. We hear them every day. They're about as subtle as a Mack truck.

"Our son is only seven, but you ought to

see him on his PC. Wow! The kid's a whiz."

"We've decided that our preschooler needs to get serious about the future, so we've got her into dance and modeling classes. After all, the possibilities are endless once she gets into making commercials."

"We think Timmy has real athletic ability. We've talked him into that basketball clinic for nine-year-olds. The pros will want the kid before long!"

Don't get me wrong. I believe deeply in the importance of parents' seeing potential and being there as an encouragement ... but to push for too much, too fast, too early takes away the fun of growing up ... of being just a relaxed, tightly knit family with well-developed, close relationships.

Take it easy! Much of what parents push for will naturally flow in time. Put your energy into cultivating close relationships. Those high-powered goals have a way of emerging at the right time.

WHY THE RIGIDITY?

There is an equally disturbing concern of mine that is robbing fun from families— rigidity. What makes this one especially subtle is that it is present in homes of well-meaning Christian parents. Wanting to guard their children from the pitfalls of a permissive, godless society, they push the pendulum to the opposite extreme. For all the right reasons, these parents decide to put the clamps on all liberty. A willingness to listen, to reason, to give a little, to shrug and pass certain things off as part of growing up is considered too permissive. In place of all that is the erection of a brick fortress, where unbending rules are adhered to and non-negotiables are regularly spelled out by super-intense parents.

Those who have bought into that family-fortress mentality won't like the following quotation. Unfortunately, those who need it the most tend to believe it the least.

> A rigid status quo orientation is indicative of pathology.... Given the continuing shifts in age, family composition and the need for redefinition of rules in families, a family locked into a rigid equilibrium ... is in trouble.
>
> ...The most viable family systems [are those where there is] a more free-flowing balance ... successful negotiation; positive and negative feedback ... with few implicit rules and more explicit rules.[4]

One major reason our family has remained close through each stage, and to this day continues to grow together and have fun together, has been our commitment to staying flexible. I hesitate to speak of this lest it all suddenly screech to a halt. I'm reminded of what one whale said to his mate, "Better watch it; when you get to the top and start to blow, that's when you get harpooned!"

My desire is neither to "blow" as if we've arrived, nor to shame those who are struggling through times of family turmoil. The only reason I return to the song of the Swindolls' close-knit family is to encourage you with the thought, *It can work! These things he is writing about have been proven over the years in their lives.* Trust me, we have made numerous mistakes and have frequently failed to carry out what we knew was best. Somehow we have survived, still walking in harmony. The grace of God is the main reason—plus children who have continued to forgive us, partly because they never had reasons to doubt their value in our eyes.

Let me return to this issue of domestic rigidity. Frankly, it cuts crossgrain with the magnificent grace and liberty of the gospel. Christ's death and resurrection provide the basis of the gospel. That "good news" has to do with our being liberated from bondage by His provision ... bondage to the law (which condemned us) and bondage to the power of sin (which intensified our guilt before God). Freed, we are now able to call our God *Father*, and our Savior *Friend*. What joy, what refreshing space this provides! It is like being set free from prison. Spiritually, we have moved into a realm of such ecstatic delight, the mere thought of being enslaved again is repulsive. To quote Jesus Himself:

> If therefore the Son shall make you free, you shall be free indeed (John 8:36, NASB).

Think of it! Free *indeed*. Totally and completely free in Him. At last, free to love, to serve, to laugh, to relax in His presence. Free to be all we were designed to be. Free to share openly ... free to think, to create, to call Him our Friend!

My question is obvious. If that is true of our condition in God's heavenly family, why shouldn't it be true in our earthly family? What keeps us from that level of spontaneity, closeness, and hilarious joy? Who came along and stole the joy from the family ... especially the Christian family? Who had the audacity to shove us back behind the bars of a relational prison? I say, *out* with such enemies of freedom!

If you know your Bible, you know which New Testament letter I have on my mind right now: Galatians. It is only six chapters long—less than 150 verses—but it packs a wallop. Paul wrote it because a group of Judaistic legalists had moved in on this congregation and stolen their liberty. He decided to expose the false teacher and exhort the Galatian Christians to break the bonds that were slowly but surely enslaving them.

Rather than my quoting passage after

passage, I encourage you to take the time to read the Galatian letter in one sitting. You'll get the picture. My purpose in mentioning it is that there are several analogies between living in God's family strictly by tight rules and rigid regulations and living in our earthly family the same way. My observation is that neither works. The joy, the spontaneity, and the creativity dry up. So does the fun. In either place, people exist in fear, realizing the hammer may fall at any moment. Worst of all, life gets reduced to nothing more than a grim existence, best described by the one who pictured our hurry-up lifestyle in these vivid words:

> This is the age of the half-read page,
> The quick hash and the mad dash,
> The bright night with the nerves
>   tight,
> The plane hop with the brief stop;
> The lamp tan in a short span,
> The big shot in a good spot,
> The brain strain and the heart pain,
> The catnaps until the spring snaps;
> And the fun is gone.[5]

Children are a lot like chickens ... they need room to squawk, lay a few eggs, flap their wings, even to fly the coop. Otherwise, let me warn you, all that lid-sitting will one day explode, and you'll wish you had not taken such a protective stance.

HOW TO KEEP THE FUN
IN THE FAMILY

Some of you are sincerely interested in changing. You see that what you have been doing isn't working. You want to lighten up and let the pressure off. You've had enough of protectionism and legalism. Good for you! You're well on your way to happiness at home if that is your attitude. Let me suggest several guidelines which will help make it happen.

First, *try to be absolutely authentic.* I know that seems like a threatening thought, but it is a giant step toward open communication.

How does authenticity reveal itself? It isn't that difficult.

- If you aren't sure of yourself, admit it.
- If you're afraid of the risk, say so.
- If you don't know the answer to a question your teenager asks you, use those wonderfully relieving words, "I don't know."
- If you were wrong, confess it.
- If you feel under pressure from others, own up to it.
- If your kids ask why, refuse to dodge behind that favorite of all parental clichés, "Because I said so." Be painfully honest with yourself. If you cannot think of a reason, maybe that's

God's way of saying you need to
bend and even give in.

Our youngsters (and oldsters) deserve
to know the truth . . . even if *we* were not
raised in such a vulnerable environment.
One father describes it this way:

> The speech was finished and the audi-
> ence had been generous with its
> applause, and in the car on the way
> home my 14-year-old son turned to me
> and said: "I really admire you, Dad,
> being able to get up there and give a
> speech like that. You always know what
> to say to people. You always seem to
> know what you're doing."
>
> I smiled when he said that. I may even
> have blushed modestly. But, at that
> moment, I didn't know what to say at all.
>
> After a while I thanked him and assured
> him that some day he would be comfort-
> able speaking in front of an audience,
> that he would always know what to say
> to people, that he would always know
> what he was doing. But what I really
> wanted to say to my son was that his
> father was not at all what he appeared to
> be and that being a man is frequently a
> facade.
>
> It has taken me a long time to admit
> that—even to myself. Especially to
> myself. *My* father, after all, really *had*
> always known what *he* was doing. He
> was strong and confident and he never
> felt pain, never knew fear. There wasn't a

leaky faucet he couldn't fix or an engine he couldn't manage to get running again. Mechanics never fooled him, salesmen never conned him. He was always calm in emergencies, always cool under fire. He never cried.

For a long time I wondered how such a man could have produced such a weakling for a son. I wondered where the self-doubts and the fears I felt all the time had come from. I wondered why the faucets I fixed always dripped twice as fast after I got finished with them, why engines that sputtered before I started to work on them went stone-dead under my wrench. I dreaded the thought that some day my father would see me cry. I didn't realize that fathers are not always everything they seem to be.

It's different for fathers than it is for mothers. Motherhood is honest, close to the surface. Mothers don't have to hide what they feel. They don't have to pretend.

When there are sounds downstairs in the middle of the night, a mother is allowed to pull the covers over her head and hope that they will go away. A father is supposed to put on his slippers and robe and march boldly down the stairs, even if he's pretty sure that it's the Manson family waiting for him in the kitchen.

When the road signs are confusing and the scenery is starting to look awfully unfamiliar, it's perfectly natural for a mother to pull over to the side of the road and ask for directions from the first person who comes along. A father is supposed to know exactly where he's going, even if he has to drive 200 miles out of the way to prove it.

Mothers can bang a new jar of peanut butter on the floor until the lid is loose enough to turn. Fathers are supposed to twist it off with their bare hands—without getting red in the face.

Mothers who lose their jobs are unfortunate. Fathers who lose their jobs are failures.

When a mother gets hurt she may want to swear, but she is only allowed to cry. When a father gets hurt he may want to cry, but he is only allowed to swear....

I should have told him that the only reason his father, like lots of fathers, doesn't admit his weaknesses is because he is afraid that someone will think he is not a real man.

More important, what I should have said to my 14-year-old son in the car that night is that someday, when he's a father, he'll feel fear and self-doubt and pain, and that it's all right. But my father never told me, and I haven't told my son.[6]

Second, *keep the rules and policies to a bare minimum.* This is especially true as the children get older. Younger children need the security of knowing where the boundaries are. That's the basis of discipline. But as little ones grow and begin to show healthy signs of exerting their independence, let it happen. Add more flex. Keep an open mind. I am not suggesting that you compromise on issues of integrity or purity. Of course not! There are limits.

I heard of a set of parents who decided they would take a hands-off policy once their son graduated from high school. He chose to stay home, commute to a local college, and continue to live off the folks' income. They agreed. He didn't work. They picked up the tab. Mom continued to make his bed and clean his room. Dad provided him with a car, a gasoline credit card, covered all his insurance expenses. It should not surprise you to read that by the end of his freshman year he was doing drugs ("just so you keep all that stuff in your room"), and bringing home one girl after another for overnight sex without once being confronted or told no. *That is ridiculous!* Giving room to grow is one thing. Giving up all moral restrictions and personal convictions for the sake of "peace at any price" is another thing entirely.

My point here has to do with adding the oil of wisdom to the gears of relationships. As children grow older and begin to think for themselves, wise parents realize that more rules and longer lists of policies only antagonize. Kids lose respect for parents who refuse to discuss reasons and never negotiate the rules.

As our children began to date, we found it necessary to establish times and places. They were expected to tell us where they were going and when they would be returning. We made it clear that if something kept them from getting to the previously stated place or being home by the agreed-upon time, a phone call was expected ... even if it meant pulling off the freeway on the way home and finding a public phone to call us. Only on the rarest occasions was that simple policy unworkable. As they grew older, a later time to return home was permitted, but the phone call remained firm. We explained it was a matter of courtesy, not distrust. When two of our children married, we found it interesting that they were so accustomed to that communication accountability they continued the habit. They now call their mates when they are going to be later than expected. The "rule" has become a way of life, which is the mark of a workable rule.

Third, *unless it is absolutely impossible to do so, say yes.* That may sound like a funny statement until you think it through. The average parental reaction is no. Regardless of the question kids ask, most parents think *no* more often than *yes.* So Cynthia and I developed a policy early on that we'd think yes ... and only when we found ourselves absolutely unable to say yes would we be forced to say no.

It is amazing how much of a positive influence that simple guideline provided for our home. I can testify that it revolutionized my attitude. Let me give you some examples.

"Can we sleep outside tonight?" Normally, like all dads, I would think and say "No." In my mind would be all kinds of airtight reasons: "The mosquitoes ..." or "You'll need to go to the bathroom and the door will be locked" or "What if it rains?" you know, dumb stuff. No longer. Sleeping outside became fine and dandy. I got to where I *preferred* 'em out there!

Another was "Can we sleep in our clothes?" Why not? (Who really cares *what* kids sleep in?) As my wife finally observed, once you have four, you're so grateful they're in bed, what they wear is of absolutely no consequence.

Another: "Can we have a party?" Sure. "How about a two-day party?" Have it! We taught them that the privilege of having a party included the responsibility of cleaning up after it ... which was perfectly okay with them. The atmosphere became more and more fun, which is what family living is all about, right?

Say yes just as often as you can.

Fourth, *a failure is not the end of the world.* When relationships are valued, when having fun is important, when saying yes is emphasized, there is risk involved. There will be times when a rule is inadvertently broken—a failure in the system occurs. So it goes. If it was accidental, welcome to the human race. Forgiveness follows confession. No grudges. And, I hope (if Dad stays quiet like he should), no lectures. If the rule was broken on purpose, that is another matter and is dealt with (privately) in a much more serious manner.

Nevertheless, any home that is run on the grace principle must have what our family calls "wobble room." Things don't always run to perfection, but the main issue is the attitude. A submissive, absolutely honest admission with a repentant spirit earns a lot of points in the Swindoll abode.

All of us mean well at the start of any plan, but the human element, being what it is, can't help but slip in occasionally. It's like the following diet plan someone passed on to me last year.

The Stress Diet

Breakfast
1/2 grapefruit
1 piece of whole-wheat toast
8 oz. skim milk

Lunch
4 oz. lean broiled chicken breast
1 cup steamed zucchini

1 Oreo cookie
Herb tea

Mid-afternoon snack
Rest of the package of Oreo cookies
1 qt. rocky road ice cream
1 jar hot fudge

Dinner
2 loaves garlic bread
Large mushroom and pepperoni pizza
Large pitcher root beer
3 Milky Ways
Entire frozen cheesecake, eaten directly
   from the freezer

That smile looks good on your face.
Your family needs to see it more often!

FLEX THOSE FUN MUSCLES!

If you have stayed with me until now,
you are to be commended. Ultra-rigid parents have probably stopped reading and
have started writing me a letter of disagreement!

Would you like two or three ideas for
developing your "flex" muscles? If so, here
they are.

*1. When the family is young, balance the tighter rules
with a strong emphasis on trust.*

Our kids need to know we trust them,
want only the best for them, believe in them.
Rather than viewing them with suspicion
and sneaking around like a CIA spy, we need
to convey our confidence in their loyalty.

That's what grace is all about. Furthermore, children flourish in such a setting. This is a good time to add that the difference between "principles" and "rules" is radical. Rules can be made and therefore reshaped or broken. Principles cannot be arbitrarily made ... they must never be broken. Rules are temporal, principles are eternal. Rules are helpful, principles are essential. Wise are the parents who understand those distinctions.

> *2. As time passes, deliberately relax more and release the controls.*

Yes, that's a risk. Yes, it's hard to do. But it won't get easier if you wait until they turn twenty! I think it would be great if parents would actually write out a "declaration of independence" for each one of the kids and hand it to them at a time when they reach a level of maturity and can handle it, like at graduation from high school or some such event.

> *3. Throughout the process, cultivate and value the importance of close relationships.*

Remember my earlier comment about every phone booth in the world being suddenly occupied if we had only five minutes to live? It's true. Nothing, absolutely *nothing* on this earth is more important to us when the chips are down than the members of our family. Do everything possible to cultivate those relationships.

Author J. Allan Petersen, writing on this

very subject, tells of a traumatic experience he endured that drilled this fact home. It happened on an airplane.

What do you think would be your last thought, your last unscheduled thought and word if you knew that in a minute or two your life was over. . . .

Let's put this in context. . . .

Every nook and cranny of the big 747 was crowded. It took off in the middle of the night in Brazil where I'd been speaking. As it moved into the night I began to doze. I don't know how long I slept, but I was starting to wake when I heard a strong voice announcing. "We have a very serious emergency." Three engines had gone because of fuel contamination, and the other engine would go any second.

The steward said in English, "Now you must do exactly as we tell you. Don't anyone think of doing anything we do not suggest. Your life depends on us. We are trained for your safety, so you must do exactly as we tell you."

Then he rattled this off in Portuguese. Everybody looked soberly at one another.

The steward said, "Now pull down the curtains, in a few minutes we are going to turn off all the lights."

My thought exclaimed, "Lord."

The plane veered and banked, as the crew tried to get it back to the airport.

The steward ran up and down the aisle and barked out orders, "Now take that card out of the seat pocket, and I want you to look at this diagram." You know, I've flown millions of miles over the world and here I thought I had the card memorized, but I panicked because I couldn't find the crazy card. Everybody looked stunned as we felt the plane plunge down.

Finally, the steward said, "Now tighten the seat belts as tight as you can, and pull up your legs and bury your head in your lap." We couldn't look out to see where we were—high or low.

I peeked around—the Portuguese were crossing themselves, and I thought, "This is it. This is serious. I can't believe this. I didn't know this was going to happen tonight. I guess this is it." And I had a crazy sensation.

Then the steward's voice broke into my consciousness, barking out in this machine-gun fashion, "Prepare for impact." Frankly, I wasn't thinking about the photocopier. I wasn't worried about the oil in my car. At times like that, involuntarily, from deep inside of us, something comes out that's never structured, planned or rehearsed. And all I could do was pray. Everybody started to pray. I found myself praying in a way I never thought of doing. As I buried my head in my lap and pulled my knees up, as I was convinced was over I said, "Oh, God, thank you. Thank you for the incredible privilege of knowing you. Life has been wonderful." And as the plane was going down my last thought, my last cry, "Oh, God, my wife! My children!

Now I should say for the sake of you the reader that I survived! As I wandered about in the middle of the night in the airport with a knot in my stomach and cotton in my mouth, I couldn't speak. I ached all over.

I thought, "What did I do? What did I say? What were my last thoughts? Why did I think that?" I wondered, "What was the bottom line?"

Here's the bottom line: relationship.

When I . . . saw my wife at the airport, I looked at her and rushed to hold her hand. I just looked at her a moment then threw my arms around her and said, "Oh, I appreciate you." And then with tears in my eyes, I looked at her again, and said, "I appreciate you so much. I didn't know if I'd ever see you again; oh, I appreciate you."

When I arrived home, I found my three sons and said, "I appreciate you. Boy, I'm glad you're in this house and I'm a part of you."

I am only one, you are only one. But because we are in a family we hold a piece of the puzzle in our own power. And what we can do, we should do. I trust that you will say with me, "And by the grace of God, I will do what I can do in my home."[7]

If you are getting caught in the squirrel cage of a hurry-up lifestyle, let me urge you to slow it down and get off. Your family deserves more than the leftovers of your time. By the grace of God do what you can do.

Start today. Please.

---

[1] David Elkind, *The Hurried Child* (Menlo Park, Calif.: Addison-Wesley Publishing Co., 1981).

[2] Susan Ferraro. "Hotsy Totsy," *American Way*, inflight magazine of American Airlines, April 1981, 61. Used by permission of the author.

[3] Reprinted courtesy of *Sports Illustrated* from the 22 February 1988 issue. © 1988, Time Inc. "Bred to Be a Superstar" by Douglas S. Looney. All rights reserved. Used by permission.

[4] David H. Olson. Douglas H. Sprenkle, and Candyce Russell, "Circumplex Model of Marital and Family Systems," *Family Process* 18 (March 1979): 12–13.

[5] From an unpublished message by Ray Stedman, senior pastor, Peninsula Bible Church, Palo Alto, Calif.

[6] D. L. Stewart, "Why Fathers Hide Their Feelings," *Redbook*, January 1985, 32. Used by permission of the author.

[7] J. Allan Petersen, "Expressing Appreciation," chapter 4 in *Family Building*, ed. Dr. George Rekers (Ventura, Calif.: Regal Books, 1985), 103–6.

Other booklets by Chuck Swindoll:

Anger

Attitudes

Commitment

Dealing with Defiance

Demonism

Destiny

Divorce

Eternal Security

God's Will

Hope

Impossibilities

Integrity

Leisure

The Lonely Whine of the Top Dog

Moral Purity

Our Mediator

Peace . . . in Spite of Panic

The Power of a Promise

Prayer

Sensuality

Singleness

Stress

This is No Time for Wimps!

Tongues

When Your Comfort Zone Gets the Squeeze

Woman